Eleanor Roosevelt

A Life of Happiness and Tears

AMERICAN
CAVALCADE

Eleanor Roosevelt

A Life of Happiness and Tears

WILLIAM JAY
JACOBS

MARSHALL CAVENDISH
CORPORATION

GREY CASTLE PRESS

Published by Grey Castle Press, Lakeville, Connecticut.

Marshall Cavendish Edition, North Bellmore, New York.

Printed in the USA.

Library of Congress Cataloging-in-Publication Data

Jacobs, William Jay.
  Eleanor Roosevelt : a life of happiness and tears / by William Jay Jacobs.
    p.   cm.— (American cavalcade)
  Reprint. Originally published : New York : Putnam, 1981.
  Includes bibliographical references (p.) and index.
  Summary: A biography of the First Lady who, despite her shyness, followed her conscience and devoted her life to helping others and working for peace.
    ISBN 1-55905-095-0 (lg. print)
    1. Roosevelt, Eleanor, 1884–1962—Juvenile literature.   2. Roosevelt, Franklin D. (Franklin Delano), 1882–1945—Juvenile literature.   3. Presidents—United States—Wives—Biography—Juvenile literature.   4. Large type books. [1. Roosevelt, Eleanor, 1884–1962.   2. First ladies.   3. Large type books.]   I. Title.   II. Series.
[E807.1R48J32 1991]
973.917'092—dc20
[B]
[92]   90-48974
                                                                                      CIP
                                                                                       AC

ISBN 1-55905-095-0
      1-55905-100-0 (set)

Photo Credits:

Cover: Brown Brothers
Franklin D. Roosevelt Library—pgs. 11, 13, 27, 83, 107, 114
Spitta, Courtesy of Franklin D. Roosevelt Library—pg. 120
The Bettmann Archive—pgs. 41, 45, 98
AP/Wide World—pgs. 73, 100
Brown Brothers—pg. 89

Contents

★

PART ONE

Challenge

The Ugly Duckling
(1884–1894)

ONCE THERE WAS a child who seemed to have everything. Born in a fine town house in New York City, she spent summers and weekends at Tivoli, her family's elegant mansion along the Hudson River. She had a pony of her own, went to fashionable parties, and even traveled across the sea in a luxurious ocean liner. A servant took care of her needs and taught her to speak French. Her beautiful mother, Anna, wore sparkling jewels and soft clothing that the little girl loved to touch and stroke.

Elliot, the little girl's father—tall, handsome, smiling—liked to play polo, to sail, to play tennis and to hunt. Once he traveled to far-away India just to hunt tigers. He had his own hunting lodge. Because he enjoyed sports and told such amusing stories, people liked to be with him. He was very popular. What's more, he adored his little daughter, whose name was Eleanor—Eleanor Roosevelt.

For many years the Roosevelt family in America had been respected and admired. They were listed among the ''Four Hundred'' families of New York—the wealthy, proud old families who thought of themselves as an aristocracy, ''the best.'' Elliott's older brother, Theodore Roosevelt, later became President of the United States.

One might think that Eleanor, with all her advantages, would have been very happy. But she was not. Instead, she later remembered her childhood as sad and lonely.

Her birthday was October 11, 1884. And almost from that very first day people remarked that she was not a good-looking child, even worse-looking than most newborn babies. Besides, her parents had wanted a boy. They could not always hide their disappointment.

As Eleanor grew older she noticed her mother's breathtaking beauty. She saw that her mother's sisters, her aunts, were very pretty, too. But she was not. She was plain, ordinary. For a while, to straighten a crooked

Anna Hall and Elliott Roosevelt, Eleanor's parents were listed among the ''Four Hundred'' wealthy and proud old families of New York.

spine, she had to wear a bulky brace on her back. Once, one of her aunts said to her face that in a family of great beauty she, Eleanor, was "the ugly duckling." The remark made her miserable, and she never forgot it.

Sometimes Eleanor would stand outside the door of her glamorous mother's room, a finger in her mouth, waiting to be asked in. Finally her mother would call out, "You may come in now, Granny." Mrs. Roosevelt called Eleanor "Granny" because she seemed to her such an old-fashioned, serious little girl.

Eleanor had two younger brothers, Elliott and Hall. She watched with envy as her mother held them in her lap and smoothed their hair. For them, there was warmth and love; for her, she later recalled, only coolness.

Knowing that she could never win praise for her beauty, Eleanor tried to do other things. She tried to have good manners so that people would like her. She tried to be a good student in school. What she wanted, most of all, was for people to notice her—to give her attention—and to admire her.

Even if Eleanor's mother was disappointed in her, her father always seemed to care. He used to dance with her, picking her up and

Eleanor, pictured here at age 3, was considered a plain and ordinary child by some family members.

throwing her into the air while she laughed and laughed. He called her his "little golden hair" or "darling little Nell."

As a child Eleanor had many fears. Once, when she was two and a half years old, the ship she was on had an accident at sea. She had to be taken off in a lifeboat. After that she was afraid of the sea. But she also was afraid of the dark, afraid of dogs, afraid of snakes, afraid of horses, afraid of being scolded, afraid of other children, afraid of strangers, afraid that people would not like her. She was a frightened, lonely little girl.

The one bright spot for her in those early years was her father. Then, when she was six, he too was taken away from her. At the time she didn't know why, except that he was ill and had to go away to get well. The truth was that he had begun drinking heavily. His condition had become so serious that he had to go to a sanitarium in a small town in Virginia where alcoholics were treated.

Eleanor, wrenched from the only person who showed her love, missed him terribly.

He wrote to her, trying to explain. "My darling little Nell," he once soothed. "Because father is not with you is not because he doesn't

love you. For I love you tenderly and dearly—
and maybe soon I'll come back well and strong
and we will have such good times together,
like we used to have.''

But, except for short visits, he never really
did come back.

Meanwhile, Eleanor's mother also became
ill. She had painful headaches. Nothing
seemed to help except for little Eleanor to hold
her head in her lap and, for hours at a time, to
stroke her forehead. It was almost as if Eleanor's hands had a magical healing power. At
those times Eleanor could not help remembering how her mother had called her ''Granny''
and been ashamed of her looks, how sometimes she had snapped at her impatiently. But
even at age seven, Eleanor was pleased to be
of use to another person. She could help her
mother and was glad to be needed.

Then, the next year, when Eleanor was
eight, disaster struck. Her mother became ill
with diphtheria and died. Her brother Elliott
caught diphtheria, and he died, too. Eleanor
and her baby brother, Hall, were taken to live
with their grandmother in her brownstone
house on Thirty-seventh Street in Manhattan.

At first, after her mother's death, Eleanor

thought she would be able to see her father more often. But that did not happen. She waited for him to return, longed for his letters. Once, Eleanor found out that he had hurt his foot and was in great pain. She wept for him, as she later came to weep for other people who suffered. But her tears did not bring him back.

Eleanor's father promised that someday they would have a home together again, would travel together. He told her to write to him often, and of course Eleanor, a dutiful child, did. He told her to be a brave girl, not to give any trouble, to become well educated, and to grow up into a woman he could be proud of.

Eleanor carried his letters with her ever afterward. And, in a way, her life became very much like the picture he painted for her.

Time and again, Eleanor's father pleaded with Grandmother Hall, asking her to let him come home and take care of his children. But she always refused. She and Eleanor's uncle Theodore Roosevelt—the same Theodore Roosevelt who later became President of the United States—thought that he could never stop drinking. They thought that having him around would be bad for such young children.

He begged, saying that if he had to stay away longer it would break his heart, but Grandmother Hall and Uncle Theodore would not change their minds. Nor did they have to. After the death of Eleanor's mother the courts had ruled that Grandmother Hall and Uncle Theodore—not the children's real father, Elliott—were to be guardians for little Eleanor and Hall. Elliott was judged "unfit" to take care of them.

As boys, Elliott and his older brother, Theodore, had competed at everything—wrestling, boxing, sailing, swimming, running, and shooting. But as they grew up Theodore worked hard at being "best" in whatever he did. Elliott, on the other hand, tried to succeed by charming people and pleasing them. Warm and generous, he usually failed to finish what he started, and never found a real career for himself.

Sometimes Eleanor's father would come to visit her in New York or, in the summer, in Grandmother Hall's fourteen-bedroom mansion at Tivoli along the Hudson. Eleanor would run down the stairs to the living room and leap into his arms. Then he would take her for a carriage ride. He drove very fast, and often she was afraid. But at the time those carriage rides were the most important thing in Eleanor's life. She gloried in them and in the chance to be with her father. More and more, hers was a dream world in which she and her father lived together and had a life of their own. To her, he seemed the most gallant, generous and loyal of men.

Eleanor knew that her mother had not believed those things. She remembered her mother speaking of him as weak-willed, a person who could not control himself—a person who did not live up to his promises. True, Eleanor remembered that sometimes he had promised to visit and had not come while she waited and waited, her hands folded on her lap, dressed in her very best clothes. Once he had come and then had to be carried drunk from the house. But to Eleanor those things did not matter. She worshiped her father, adored him, struggled to please him.

In August, 1894—at the age of thirty-four—Elliott Roosevelt, the father of Eleanor Roosevelt, died. At the time, Eleanor was ten years old. Within eighteen months she had lost her mother, a brother and, finally, her dear father.

Grandmother Hall decided that Eleanor should not go to the funeral. She was, said Grandmother Hall, too young to deal with death. And perhaps that was best for Eleanor. She could always remember her father as he was in her dreams—never really dead and buried, but alive, exciting, smiling, reaching out to her.

Now Eleanor had a goal in life. It was to prove that her mother and all the others who had criticized her father had been wrong. She would prove that in her own life—by living as he had asked her to. She would be brave and good and strong and true. She would help other people. She would live a life that would make him proud of her.

Becoming a Swan
(1894–1902)

FOR MANY MONTHS after her father's death Eleanor pretended that he was still alive and she could speak to him. She made him the hero of stories she wrote for school. Instead of making friends she sat in her room and read. Often she just cried. Nothing that Grandmother Hall and her aunts did for her seemed to help. She was lonely and unhappy.

The house on Thirty-seventh Street made life even more dreadful. It was dark and gloomy, with no place for her to play. The family took their meals together, but ate in complete silence. Eleanor's governess, Madeleine, used to scream at her and—for fun—pull her hair to make her cry. But Eleanor was too terrified of Madeleine to tell Grandmother Hall about her. An even more frightening thing was happening. Eleanor's Uncle Vallie, one of Grandmother Hall's sons, who had taught her horseback riding and been kind to her, now was beginning to drink heavily. Sometimes he was violent, and she was afraid that, while drunk, he might hurt her.

Grandmother Hall had trouble controlling Vallie and her other children—Eleanor's aunts Maude and Edith ("Pussie"), and her Uncle Eddie. Exceptionally beautiful and wealthy, descended from the Livingstons, one of America's most famous families, Grandmother Hall was a widow. She had been pampered and spoiled from childhood, accustomed to being cared for in every way. After her husband's death, with no real experience in the world, she was helpless, confused. Her daughter Anna—Eleanor's mother—really was in charge of the family's affairs, even after Anna's marriage to Elliott Roosevelt.

Then, following Anna's death, Grandmother Hall tried to do for her grandchildren what she had failed to do with her own children—make them live up to her rules. Every morning Eleanor and Hall were supposed to take cold baths for their health—something Eleanor usually got around by secretly adding hot water to the tub. For good posture Eleanor had to walk with her arms behind her back, clamped over a walking stick. On Sundays she was not allowed to play games.

Like many wealthy women of that time, Grandmother Hall did not believe that girls needed much education except in such matters as dancing and sewing. She had given Eleanor's mother, Anna, little formal schooling. Eleanor, in turn, could barely read and write by the age of seven, although she had been given some lessons in speaking French (the language of "culture") and in memorizing parts of the New Testament, also in French. By the age of ten, when she came to live with Grandmother Hall, she would have been in the fifth grade of most schools, but actually was far behind.

Still, she liked to read, and she asked question after question. Her mother had made over some of the upstairs rooms in their New York town house into schoolrooms, hired two teachers, and invited in the daughters of other wealthy families. Grandmother Hall decided to keep the little school going.

Eleanor took her schoolwork seriously, just as her father had wanted her to. Some of the students at school called her a "grind." They said that all she ever did was study. Probably it was true. Partly that was because she was ambitious. She really wanted to learn. Besides, she knew that if she were a good student people would notice her. They would praise her and admire her. More than anything else, that was what she wanted—and needed.

Sometimes Eleanor did have fun. She especially liked to visit with her Uncle Theodore Roosevelt, at Oyster Bay, Long Island. He loved all of his nieces and nephews, but probably she was his favorite—the sad, serious daughter of his unfortunate brother, Elliott. Visits with Uncle Ted always meant games to play and romping outdoors with the many Roosevelt children.

Eleanor never forgot how Uncle Ted threw her into the water to teach her how to swim. She started to sink, and he had to fish her out. He used to read to the children old Norse tales and poetry. It was from Uncle Ted that Eleanor first learned how much fun it could be to read books aloud.

Even at Sagamore Hill, Uncle Ted's home, she couldn't completely escape her unhappiness. Once, Grandmother Hall sent her to a party there in a white dress with blue bows on each shoulder. When she put on the dress the hem hung above her knees, like a little girl's party dress, although she was fourteen at the time. She was painfully embarrassed. Her cousin, Alice Roosevelt, offered to lend her a dress, but Eleanor, too proud to accept, just suffered.

In school, Eleanor once spilled ink over her dress. Because she had only one other school dress, and it was in the wash, she had to wear the same dress to class the next day with the enormous ink stains showing. Grandmother Hall had plenty of money of her own, and Eleanor's parents had left her with trust funds which should have paid for her food and clothing, but Grandmother Hall, growing old, often became confused about things. With Vallie's drinking problem on her mind, there was little time left to think of Eleanor and Hall. Nor was she really warm or affectionate with them. Largely, they were just neglected.

When Eleanor was about to turn fifteen, Grandmother Hall decided that it would be best for her to go away to boarding school in England. The school she chose was Allenswood, near Wimbledon Common, on the outskirts of London.

At Allenswood Eleanor got a fresh start in life. She began to gain confidence in herself. For the first time she could secretly hope that perhaps, after all, she might cease to be an "ugly duckling" and grow up to be a swan.

In its strict discipline Allenswood was like many other English private schools. The girls—it was, of course, an all-girls school— had responsibilities. They had to make their own beds and keep their rooms neat. Teachers could inspect their closets and chests of drawers at any time to be sure their clothes were in order. At mealtimes they had to have perfect table manners. Any food they took on their plates had to be eaten. After breakfast they all had to take a brisk walk outdoors, no matter how miserable the weather.

For two hours each day they had to play an outdoor sport. Eleanor was not very good at sports, so she dreaded the thought of this. But she chose field hockey, and, since it was her duty to play, she kept at it. Duty was impor- tant to Eleanor. She tried as hard as she could. When, at last, she made the first team she was very proud.

Every day, too, she took an ice-cold shower and did vigorous exercises. Those things, Eleanor thought, would toughen her, steel her, make her stronger as a person.

But it was not ice-cold showers or sports that turned Eleanor's life around. It was Allenswood's remarkable headmistress, a Frenchwoman named Mademoiselle Marie Souvestre. Mademoiselle Souvestre taught the school's classes in French literature and English history. But, using her own life as a model, she taught the girls much more important things too.

Mademoiselle Souvestre was interested in the arts. She was interested in politics. And she was deeply interested in bringing about justice—fairness—in an unfair world. Often in class she would discuss the case of Captain Dreyfus, a Jew. In 1894 the French government had sentenced Dreyfus to the living death of imprisonment on Devil's Island, off the coast of South America, for a crime that, it was later proved he had never committed. Mademoiselle was one of those who championed his cause. She also believed that Great Britain was wrong to make war on the helpless Boers (Dutch) of South Africa. It was from Mademoiselle that Eleanor learned to stand up and fight for the underdog—for the rights of suffering people who could not fight for themselves.

Eleanor (top row, third from right) attended the Allenswood boarding school in England beginning in 1899. The head-mistress, Mlle. Marie Souvestre, helped shape Eleanor's political and social views.

Mademoiselle insisted that the girls think for themselves, not just accept the ideas of their friends and teachers. A student never could please her just by spitting back on tests the words that she had said. That only made her angry. Each girl had to use her mind, apply herself, *discover* the truth. And to Mademoiselle nothing could be true unless it was also fair—unless it was right, in a person's heart.

Schooling at Allenswood was, then, much more than an exercise. It was preparation for a life of service. Mademoiselle made her students feel that each of them had a responsibility somehow to leave the world better than they found it. That was the real purpose of education: to build a storehouse of knowledge that they could use in helping others.

Like no other teacher at Allenswood Mademoiselle aroused her students. She interested them. She made them feel that life was fun—that it was filled with endlessly exciting things to see and to do. After studying with her, one never again could think of life as dull.

Mademoiselle Souvestre (sometimes people called her ''Sou'') was the most important person in Eleanor's early life, besides her father, of course. Mademoiselle took an interest in her as a person, not just as a student. Once, Eleanor was spending a school vacation in France with an Allenswood friend, learning to speak the language better by living with a French family. Mademoiselle arranged to have a new dress made for her. It was a red dress, one that many years later her friend still remembered. After all the old, worn dresses that Grandmother Hall had given to her to wear, it made her feel proud of herself.

One of the other Allenswood teachers helped her stop the habit of chewing her fingernails. The teacher reminded Eleanor that her father always wanted her to look her best, to be well groomed. She agreed to try. From that time on, she never chewed her fingernails. And she took more interest in her appearance.

At Allenswood Eleanor learned to take care of her health. She learned to eat nutritious foods and to get plenty of sleep, as well as to exercise.

Eleanor also learned that, as Uncle Theodore liked to say, if you make those around you happy you will become happy, too. She practiced being good in every possible way. And, for the first time, people didn't tease her about being a "goody-goody." They returned her love. They called her by the nickname given to her by her Hall aunts, "Totty," and really came to like her. Every Saturday, the girls used to put a book or flowers in the room of another girl they admired. Sometimes Eleanor would return to her room to find it filled with flowers.

What a difference from her sad, lonely days with Grandmother Hall after her father's death!

Gradually, Eleanor began to feel that she could do things on her own. When she was sixteen, Grandmother Hall agreed to let her go on an extended trip to Europe with Mademoiselle Souvestre. Eleanor planned all of the details herself—the train schedules, the hotels, the packing. She and Mademoiselle would stop along the way, whenever they were ready, for a meal of bread and cheese and coffee. When it pleased them they would go off to visit a church or see a painting. In Florence, Eleanor saw the city on her own, walking to every church, every museum.

She was sixteen—alive to beauty, alive to the awakening sense of her own womanhood.

Eleanor Roosevelt was growing up. And a sense of joy welled up inside her.

3

Courtship and Marriage (1902–1905)

AT THE BEGINNING of 1902 Grandmother Hall told Mademoiselle Souvestre that Eleanor would not be coming back for a fourth year at Allenswood. Nearly eighteen, she was to be introduced to New York society. She was to be a debutante—to go to dances and parties and begin to take her place in the social world with other young women. Eleanor would much rather have stayed at Allenswood and then gone on to college. But at that time in her life she believed that her duty, above all, was to obey.

So Eleanor returned to Tivoli, Grandmother Hall's country home. Uncle Vallie was still drinking, perhaps even more heavily. Sometimes he would stand at a window with a rifle and shoot at visitors. Eleanor's Aunt "Pussie," whom she once considered a friend, flitted from one romance to another and sometimes threatened suicide. One day, in a fit of rage, she tried to hurt Eleanor by describing her father as a weakling whose conduct had brought shame and disgrace on the family. Tivoli, meanwhile, like the house on Thirty-seventh Street, was lonely, grim, unhappy. Once Eleanor burst into tears and fell into the arms of "Auntie Bye"— Anna Roosevelt Cowles, her father's sister— crying, "Oh, Auntie, I have no real home!"

Now that she was removed from Allenswood, Eleanor's old uncertainty about her looks came back again. She saw herself as too tall, too thin, too plain. She worried about her "buckteeth" that she thought made her look horselike. It especially hurt when she compared herself to "Princess" Alice Roosevelt, her cousin, who always could be so witty, so charming, so attractive. Eleanor tried to forget how Alice always teased her. But, really, she never could forget.

Then the round of parties began. Including Eleanor and Alice, there were five Roosevelt girls "coming out," being introduced to society as debutantes in 1902. One newspaper said of them—and probably the reporter was not thinking of Alice—that the Roosevelt girls were "interesting-looking, but they are not pretty." In those days, having to hear that kind of snippy remark was part of the ordeal of being a debutante. To Eleanor, it seemed that the girls were on exhibition, like cattle. She left most of the parties as early as was polite.

It was about then that the Junior League was becoming important. The Junior League was a club, made up of wealthy young women, that did charitable things for the poor. Members of the Junior League often worked in hospitals and in settlement houses (places where immigrants could come to learn English, or listen to music, or where the children could play games). Every debutante was added to the Junior League's membership list, but few of them actually did anything. For Eleanor, it was a perfect opportunity. It was just the kind of work that Mademoiselle Souvestre always had urged her to do. So she plunged in.

Her assignment was to work with poor children at the Rivington Street Settlement in New York's Lower East Side. She taught dancing and gymnastic exercises to the girls there. Other members of the Junior League taught classes in cooking and art. Sometimes they took children to the beach or to the country. They took them to museums and to musical performances. They also tried to get parents to help themselves: to demand shorter hours of work for women, better schools, cleaner and safer streets. Junior Leaguers urged them to stand up for their rights. They told parents to organize and go into politics to get new laws passed to protect themselves.

Sometimes there were debutante parties scheduled at the same time Eleanor had work to do at the Rivington Street Settlement. Usually she decided to go to the settlement house and miss the party. Her work became vitally important to her. It became a way for her to feel good about herself and also be useful to others. Having suffered, Eleanor could understand other people's suffering. Besides, helping them gave her pleasure.

Before long Eleanor was one of the leaders of the Junior League. True, her debutante friends giggled about her. They didn't think of her as being, like them, lighthearted and fun-loving. But even they, Eleanor soon noticed, would trust her with their secrets. They knew she was interested in them as people, would listen to them, and would not betray their trust.

Meanwhile, something wonderful happened to Eleanor. She fell in love. The young man was her fifth cousin, Franklin Delano Roosevelt.

They had known each other since childhood. Franklin recalled how once he had carried her piggy-back in the nursery. And Eleanor remembered a party when she was fourteen, skinny and shy, and he had asked her to dance. Shortly after she returned home from Allenswood they had met by chance on a train. They talked—really for the first time at any length—and liked each other.

For a while they met in secret, or at family affairs. Then they began to invite each other to parties. They walked in the woods or along the shore. They went to hayrides. In the summer of 1903 Franklin invited Eleanor several times to his family's home at Hyde Park on the Hudson, and then to their vacation home on Campobello Island, at the border between Maine and Canada.

Some of Eleanor's friends tried to discourage her from loving Franklin. They said that he was nothing but a handsome college boy, that he was not serious about life. A few members of the family considered him so shallow that they spoke of him as "the feather-duster." Alice Roosevelt said that he was "prissy" and "a good little mamma's boy." But Eleanor thought that Alice was jealous of her. As for the others, she simply refused to listen to them. It seemed to her that Franklin was deeper than he pretended to be—that really he was hiding his true feelings in order to appear light and amusing. From the beginning she believed in him. She thought he was intelligent and had good ideas. And she wanted to help him in his career.

Yet Eleanor still had doubts about herself. She was unsure. There was Franklin—tall, strong and very handsome. He was a fine athlete. Many women wanted him. Why would he choose her—"the ugly duckling"? What could she possibly bring him?

But Franklin had thought things through. He must have seen in her qualities of strength that he needed. Besides, as Eleanor looked back on the romance many years later, she guessed at other reasons: She may have seemed "safe" to him. She was simple and quiet. Yet she had a dignity that he needed in a woman. He could take her places and know that she would not be an embarrassment. She was comfortable to be with. Franklin also knew that she would let him live his life as he chose. She would be a good listener when he talked. She would not dominate him. Finally, he must have known that she would be a good mother for his children, and a wife he could count on and trust.

Still, Eleanor could not be sure. Did he really love her? Would he always? She wrote to him, quoting a poem she knew: "'. . . Unless you can swear, *"For life, for death!"*. . . . Oh, never call it loving!'"

Franklin promised that his love was, indeed, for life. And Eleanor agreed to marry him.

It was the fall of 1903. He was twenty-one. She was nineteen.

All along, Franklin's mother, Sara Delano Roosevelt, had seen what was happening between the two. And she did not like it. After the death of her husband she had devoted her whole life to Franklin. Even before that she had planned every detail of his childhood: the schools he would go to; his travel plans in Europe each summer; the parties he would attend. Nothing was left to chance. She bought the home at Campobello Island so that he could learn to sail and to love the sea. When he enrolled at Harvard College she rented a house nearby so that she could be close to him.

Franklin's decision to marry Eleanor was not part of Sara's plan for him. She had hoped to travel with him for a while after his graduation from Harvard. Then she thought they would settle down together at Hyde Park. Perhaps afterward, with her help, he might want to start a law practice, but not one that would take too much time. She really had in mind for him the life of a ''gentleman farmer,'' living in quiet comfort along the Hudson, as his ancestors had lived. After ten years or so he might think about marriage, but certainly not before then—and certainly not to someone as ordinary, as plain, as Eleanor seemed to be.

Sara fought hard to keep her hold on Franklin. At first she arranged parties where he could meet other young women. But that did not work; he insisted that Eleanor be present and always made his way back to her. Next she had him go away on a cruise to the West Indies. On the cruise he met an older woman, and they liked each other. Still, Franklin did not change his mind about marrying Eleanor.

Finally, to please his mother, he enrolled at Columbia University Law School, in New York City, so that he could be close to home. All the time he was respectful to her. He didn't disagree or argue. But he was stubborn. He simply would not give in. That often was the way he handled problems.

Meanwhile, he tried to reassure his mother. Once he wrote to her:

> . . . You know that nothing can ever change what we have always been and always will be to each other—only now you have two children to love and to love you—and Eleanor, as you know, will always be a daughter to you in every true way. . . .

At last, Sara (or "Cousin Sally," as Eleanor sometimes liked to call her) realized that Franklin would go ahead with the marriage. He would do it no matter what she said. So she, not Franklin, finally gave in.

Eleanor wanted to be her friend, wanted to be a good daughter-in-law. So she wrote to her in friendship.

> I know just how you feel & how hard it must be, but I do so want you to learn to love me a little. You must know that I will always try to do what you wish, for I have grown to love you dearly. . . .
>
> It is impossible for me to tell you how I feel toward Franklin. I can only say that my one great wish is always to prove worthy of him.

Eleanor set the wedding date for March 17, 1905, when "Uncle Ted"—by then President Theodore Roosevelt—could be present, in place of Eleanor's father, to "give the bride away."

It was a beautiful wedding. The brides-maids—and Eleanor made certain to include her cousin Alice Roosevelt among them—wore taffeta gowns. Everywhere there were white lilacs, lilies and pink rosebuds. The altar was framed in palms and pink roses. Just as Franklin wished, his old headmaster from the Groton Academy, the Reverend Endicott Peabody, waited at the altar to marry the couple.

And then it was over. They were man and wife.

On Jan. 17, 1905, Eleanor married Franklin Roosevelt in New York. The wedding date had been set to allow Uncle Ted, then President Theodore Roosevelt, to give Eleanor away in place of her father.

Their friends swirled around them, offering congratulations. "There's nothing like keeping the name in the family!" laughed Uncle Ted in his high-pitched voice. He kissed Eleanor and then was off to the dining room, where the refreshments were being served. Soon the other guests followed in his trail, attracted by his funny stories and his exciting personality. Someone later said that Uncle Ted had to be "the bride at every wedding and the corpse at every funeral." And it certainly was true that day.

Before long, Eleanor and Franklin were left standing all alone, deserted. Franklin seemed annoyed, but Eleanor didn't mind. She had found the ceremony, a religious one, deeply moving. And she stood there next to her new husband in a glow of idealism—very serious, very grave, very much in love.

She was determined to be a good wife to Franklin. She would do her duty to him. And, if she could, she would also try to relieve some of the suffering she had seen in the world.

Under a shower of rice from the wedding guests Eleanor and Franklin left for a brief honeymoon. They spent it at Franklin's home,

Hyde Park, which his mother insisted on turning over to them for the occasion. Thus, from the beginning, Sara Delano Roosevelt—''Cousin Sally''—announced that her life would be bound up with theirs.

4

*Family
(1905–1916)*

AT FIRST, Eleanor and Franklin could not take a real honeymoon. Franklin was still a student in law school and had classes to attend. But when his summer vacation came in 1905 they sailed for Europe on the *Oceanic*. Eleanor, still afraid of the sea because of her childhood experience on a passenger ship, dreaded the trip, yet wanted it very much. She told herself not to be afraid. In fact, she convinced herself so well that she was not even seasick.

Everywhere, Eleanor and Franklin stayed at the most elegant hotels and dined at the finest restaurants. Both had traveled in Europe before, and they visited many places they already had seen. But this time was different; for now they saw the old places together, hand in hand.

Eleanor and Franklin took a honeymoon trip to Europe in the summer of 1905.

Eleanor brought back fond memories of the trip: the magnificent churches and cathedrals; the great art galleries of London and Paris; and a funny gondola ride in Venice, with Franklin trying to sing like the gondolier.

There was sadness too. Eleanor visited Allenswood, but Mademoiselle Souvestre had died several weeks before. Without Sou, Eleanor found the school a bleak and lonely place.

The couple returned to a new home—a fashionable town house on East Thirty-seventh Street in New York City. Franklin's mother (or Mammá, as Eleanor had begun to call her) had rented it for them. She also had furnished it according to her own taste and even had chosen three servants to staff it. Her own home was only three blocks away.

For Eleanor, there was little housework to do. The servants took care of the cooking, cleaning and sewing. Instead she spent her time with a small group of friends. All of them were wealthy. All of them came from old established families. They were, as Mammá said, "the right people."

Every day Eleanor walked or went for a carriage ride with Mammá. She had at least one meal a day with her and played cards with her. Eleanor asked her about the details of running the household and usually followed her advice without question. Above all, Eleanor wanted to make Franklin happy. And part of the job of making him happy, she thought, was pleasing his mother—trying to win her love.

All of Eleanor's life she had taught herself to do what she ought to do. She had disciplined herself, learned self-control, learned to hold herself in check. Never would she have dreamed of saying aloud that she was ill or unhappy. Instead, she learned to suffer in silence. She learned to be a good companion to others and not to think of herself.

Pictures of Eleanor in those early years of her marriage show her as stiff, rigid, tense. Usually in the pictures she wore starched white dresses with high collars, and she looked very, very proper. "In those days," she later said, "we dressed according to the calendar, not the weather."

In May, 1906, the couple's first child was born—Anna Eleanor. As a new mother Eleanor found it hard to describe her great joy at holding her baby close and feeling the warmth of its body along-side her. Mammá had very much wanted a boy, but even she was fascinated by every movement of Anna's little fingers and toes.

During the next nine years Eleanor had five more babies: James (1907), Franklin, Jr. (who was born in January, 1909, and died seven months and nine days later), Elliott (1910), a second Franklin, Jr. (1914), and John (1916).

Mammá made the children her own, even choosing their clothes and their toys. She decided who their childhood governesses would be and which private schools they would attend. If Mammá thought one of the children needed a dose of castor oil or other medicine, Eleanor, unsure of herself, usually went along with the idea. Mammá almost always had the final word.

Occasionally Eleanor tried to be strict with the children, but her strictness never stopped them from doing mischief. Anna and James used to drop paper bags filled with water on people passing under the windows of the Roosevelts' town house. Once, some of the children threw stink bombs into a party their parents were giving.

Sometimes Eleanor had her own ideas. Believing that fresh air was good for children, she once put little Anna in a wire crib outside the window of her Thirty-seventh Street home. When neighbors threatened to report her to the Society for the Prevention of Cruelty to Children, Eleanor took the crib inside.

It was hard for Eleanor. Whenever she asked Franklin to punish the children for something they had done, he somehow managed not to do it. He could not bear to punish them. Although he loved to romp and play with them, he took little responsibility for teaching them right from wrong.

Mammá's influence was even worse. Trying to buy the children's love, she gave them money. When they were naughty she threatened to cut them out of her will. When one was especially good to her she promised that child an extra share of her wealth.

Once, when James was older, Eleanor and Franklin bought him a used car. He left the convertible top down one night, and a rainstorm completely ruined the interior. To teach him a lesson his parents refused to buy him another car. But he went to Mammá for help, and she bought him a new and better one. She once did the same for Franklin, Jr., after he had wrecked his car on a dare.

Yet Eleanor and Franklin sometimes were to blame, too. They let Mammá pay for things they could not afford—extra servants, vacations, expensive doctor bills, clothing. She offered, and they took.

One result was that the children grew up without real discipline. They didn't understand the value of money. They were unsure of themselves, since they never had to be responsible for their own actions. Somebody was always there, ready to bail them out. Among them, the Roosevelt children had a total of seventeen marriages, many ending in divorce. Living busy lives, Eleanor and Franklin undoubtedly did their best. But, as parents, they probably were too weak.

For her part, Eleanor explained that she was never good at giving advice. She believed in letting children work out their own plans, live their own lives. As she put it, it is hard for a parent to let go, to let children make their own decisions. But, said Eleanor, that is really the best way.

In those years, Eleanor never complained to Franklin about his mother. Once, however, when his mother gave them a new home next to her own, with a connecting wing, Eleanor turned to Franklin in tears. She told her husband that it was not really her home. She had not helped to plan or prepare it. And it was not the way she wanted to live.

Franklin held her close and tried to comfort her. But Eleanor understood that, most of all, he wanted no trouble between the two women in his life. He wanted to be left alone to build his career. He thought that if you ignored a problem long enough it usually would settle itself.

Eleanor began to withdraw more and more into her own private world. She tried to learn golf and tennis to please Franklin, but was not good at either sport. So she stayed on the sidelines. The most she could do with Franklin was to go on long walks or picnics. He enjoyed light talk and flirting with women. But Eleanor could not be lighthearted. She was serious, shy, easily embarrassed.

When Franklin did something Eleanor did not like, she almost never lost her temper. Instead, she bottled up her anger inside and did not talk to him at all. As he used to say, she "clammed up." And her silence only made things worse, because it puzzled him. Faced with her coldness, her brooding silence, he only grew angrier and more distant.

Franklin found the practice of law too boring. He wanted more excitement in his life. In 1910 he was elected to the New York State Senate, and he and Eleanor went to live in the state capital, Albany.

Then, in 1913, President Woodrow Wilson appointed Franklin Assistant Secretary of the Navy. Franklin and Eleanor rented a lovely little house on N Street in Washington. Mammá remained in New York, but she visited often, either in Washington or, in the summertime, at Campobello. Eleanor wrote to her frequently, still depended on her, still did as she was told.

As the wife of a high-ranking official in Washington, Eleanor was expected to make social visits. So she made them. She was expected to give parties. So she gave them. As usual, Eleanor was doing her duty, living up to other people's expectations, living up to her obligations.

People approved of Eleanor. Often her friends would remark that she and Franklin were ''the ideal couple''—the perfect pair. ''Could there be,'' they would ask, ''a better wife, a better mother, a better daughter-in-law than Eleanor Roosevelt?''

She must be, people said, among the very happiest of women.

But she was not.

5

*A Time of Testing
(1917–1918)*

IN 1914 A great war broke out in Europe. At first, England, France and Russia lined up against Germany and Austria-Hungary. Then more and more countries joined in the fight. Finally, in April, 1917, President Wilson asked the Congress of the United States to declare war. America too was drawn into the killing. It was to be, said Wilson, "a war to end wars," a war "to make the world safe for democracy."

The President's purposes were high. But to Eleanor, killing was still killing. Suffering was still suffering. At first she stood by just watching events from a distance. She read the newspapers. She went about her usual social rounds. Then she decided to do something—anything—to help.

First, she took charge of the knitting at the Navy Department's work rooms, assigning knitting jobs to volunteers and then picking up the finished work. Next, she started working at the Red Cross canteen. There she and the other volunteers gave coffee, sandwiches and soup to soldiers passing through Washington. They helped the soldiers write letters to their families. Sometimes, when the men were lonely, the volunteers danced with them, or just talked to them and tried to make them feel a little less homesick.

In all her years of marriage Eleanor had seldom kept the household accounts or balanced a checkbook. But somebody had to keep the canteen's books. So she learned accounting and did it herself. She learned to drive a car so that she could take soldiers from place to place. She began to feel more independent. Something else happened. She began to look at the world differently. Always before she had known how some people suffered. As a child traveling in Europe she once had felt sorry for a boy who, with bleeding feet, was leading her donkey along a mountain path strewn with sharp rocks; and she had come back walking beside the donkey while he rode. On her honeymoon with Franklin she had felt sorry for the third-class passengers on the *Oceanic* crammed together like cattle below-decks in the steerage compartment. Her work in the settlement house on Rivington Street had opened her eyes to still other suffering.

The difference, once the war began, was Eleanor's feeling that she actually could do something about it. She could do something to help.

Once, she visited an insane asylum that the Navy Department had taken over to treat sailors and marines shell-shocked in combat. She saw that many of the men just walked back and forth in their rooms, unattended. Some went naked. They had nothing to do— no sports, no games, no exercise. And nobody seemed to care.

Instead of just being horrified and doing nothing, as she usually had done before, Eleanor took action. After all, Franklin was Assistant Secretary of the Navy—a powerful position. So when she spoke people listened. She demanded that the Secretary of the Interior make a personal visit to the hospital. Then she got the Red Cross to agree to build a recreation room. And she insisted that the government supply newspapers, games, a phonograph and records for the room.

Eleanor had her way. Because of her action the hospital became a better place. And from this experience she had learned an important lesson. It became almost her motto that "what one has to do usually can be done." But hopes and wishes are not enough. It takes hard work to make things better in the world.

The war had awakened Eleanor to what needed to be done. And, once awake, she determined never again to go back to sleep. Ever afterward, she kept on trying to help others.

Probably it was a good thing that she had so much to think about in that autumn of 1918. Because that was the time when, as she put it, "the bottom dropped out" of her world. She discovered that Franklin had been having a love affair with her social secretary, Lucy Mercer.

Lucy Mercer was young and beautiful. Although poor, she came from one of the oldest, most respected families in Maryland. She had been married and divorced once when Eleanor hired her as a social secretary—someone to take care of her appointments and help her answer the mail. Lucy did her job well. Eleanor could depend on her. She worked long hours, often late into the evening. Mammá came to like her, too. In fact, she was almost a member of the family. The Roosevelts sometimes took her along on vacations.

By 1918 "Princess Alice"—Alice Roosevelt—was living in Washington, married to Congressman Nicholas Longworth. She knew about Franklin and Lucy Mercer. In fact, she took a fiendish glee in entertaining the two of them at lunch in her home. Someone later told Eleanor that, smiling, Alice had sniped, "Franklin deserved a little fun. After all, he's married to Eleanor."

In September, 1918, Franklin returned from a trip to Europe seriously ill. He had double pneumonia. Eleanor had to take care of his mail. And, sifting through it, she discovered Lucy's love letters to him.

Immediately Eleanor told Franklin that she knew what was going on. She said that she would agree to a divorce, but that it was up to him.

He might well have left Eleanor and married Lucy Mercer. But he didn't. Because Lucy was a Catholic she herself felt guilty about loving a married man with five children. Mammá was furious with Franklin and threatened to cut him out of her will if he divorced Eleanor.

Finally, Franklin's friend and political adviser, Louis Howe, told him that a divorce would mean the end of his political career. In those days, most people considered divorce a great failure or, even worse, a sin. It was almost impossible for a divorced man to win election to high office.

Franklin thought the situation over carefully. He decided that, ''for the good of the children,'' as he put it, he and Eleanor should stay married.

About a year and a half later Lucy Mercer married a wealthy older man, Wintie Rutherfurd.

Usually Eleanor didn't talk about such things. But, years later, she came to believe that it is best to be honest—to face facts as they are, not as one might like them to be.

Looking back on her life, Eleanor claimed to understand why Franklin might have done what he did. To her, she explained, life was something to be lived for a purpose. It was a serious matter to be gotten through with honor. Unlike Franklin, she did not like parties and dances. She left them early or did not go to them at all. He, on the other hand, was fun-loving. In those days he liked to enjoy himself at the Chevy Chase Club or the Metropolitan Club, sometimes not returning from a night out until early in the morning. Eleanor had dated few men before marrying Franklin, but he had always been popular with women.

Other conflicts arose between the two. Eleanor was on time for appointments; Franklin was almost always late. Eleanor faithfully answered letters and returned phone calls; Franklin usually let his go. Eleanor insisted on the family's bills being paid promptly; Franklin often forgot to pay them. Just as Eleanor had to prod and push her brilliant younger brother, Hall and mother him, she had to organize Franklin's personal affairs. If not, things simply weren't done.

Such differences, seemingly small, revealed a deeper clash in values and world view—a different sense of what life is all about and how it should be lived.

Eleanor and Franklin had not broken up their marriage. But Eleanor would never forget what he had done. Ten years of marriage, six babies! For all that time, as she thought of it, she had tried hard to be a loyal wife and a good mother. She had thought of nothing else but how to please him and please his mother. She had made him the purpose of her life.

And what had he done in return? He had given her great pain. He had destroyed her self-confidence, her self-respect. He had taken the anchor from her life. He had hurt her deeply.

Eleanor forgave Franklin. She agreed to go on living with him and helping him in his career.

Yet from that time on she determined to live her own life, too, to have her own freedom and independence. Things would never again be as they had been. She could forgive Franklin, but she could not forget.

Painfully, she began to pick up the pieces of her life and start out anew.

PART TWO

Response and Triumph

A Time of Growth
(1919–1928)

NOW THIRTY-FIVE years old, Eleanor looked at herself and tried to decide what to do next. For much of her life she had been dependent on other people. And those people had hurt her. Now, slowly, she began to build a new life for herself. In that new life she promised, she would rely on herself. She would turn her pain and disappointment into strength.

In 1920 the Democratic Party chose James Cox of Ohio as its candidate for the Presidency. Then, surprisingly, the party selected young Franklin Roosevelt to run for Vice-President. Week after week he campaigned: shaking hands, marching in parades, riding thousands of miles by train. Sometimes he made ten or twelve speeches in a day. All the time, Eleanor stood by his side, smiling, doing what was expected of her as a candidate's wife.

Even if she heard Franklin make the same speech several times in a day, she sat on the platform next to him listening intently to what he said. Some of the newspaper reporters teased her about being so serious. They would make funny faces at her from the audience, trying to get her to laugh. At the time Eleanor had little sense of humor. And the reporters knew it. Still, they liked her. Some of them may also have felt sorry for her.

Eleanor and Franklin both worked hard to win the election. But the Republican ticket of Harding and Coolidge won by a landslide. Nevertheless, Franklin had traveled to parts of the country he never had seen before. People got to know him. He got to know the country. Gradually he was learning to talk to many kinds of people, including laborers, farmers, and local politicians, and not just people whose lives were limited to Harvard, Hyde Park and high society.

The campaign was important for Eleanor too. For the first time she had seen how much fun politics could be. Usually Franklin had been busy planning his speeches during the day, playing poker with his friends at night. Eleanor was something of a wallflower. But Franklin's adviser, Louis Howe made friends with her. He asked her to look over Franklin's speeches, and he drew her into talks with newsmen. He respected her ideas, made her feel wanted. He made her think she had value as a person, as herself, Eleanor Roosevelt, not just Mrs. Franklin Delano Roosevelt, the candidate's wife.

In the beginning Eleanor had not liked Louis Howe. He was small and wrinkled like an old gnome. Because he smoked one cigarette after another, his clothing, which always looked as if he had slept in it, was filled with ashes and smelled musty.

But he cared about her. Perhaps he thought that a candidate's wife was important in winning votes. And Louis Howe needed votes to achieve his main ambition, to get Franklin elected President of the United States. To Louis, Franklin was a hero, handsome, athletic, charming, everything Louis was not. And Louis gave him fierce, undivided loyalty.

Whatever Louis's reasons for befriending Eleanor, he brought her out of her shell. It was Louis who taught her how to project her voice when speaking to a group. He showed her that, because she was shy and nervous, she was giggling as she spoke. And, as he explained patiently, "A lady can't laugh and talk at the same time." Eleanor's nervousness also made her speak in a shrill, high-pitched voice. He showed her how to relax and deepen her voice. Most important, he made her keep her remarks brief. His advice was, "Have something to say, say it, and sit down."

Eleanor and Louis became the closest of friends. Later, they often were the ones who sat offstage, planning, while they watched the "beautiful people," like Franklin, get the applause. In fact, Eleanor and Louis sometimes used to laugh heartily as they compared newspaper photographs; they would compete to see which of them could find an uglier photo of the other.

In the summer of 1921 the life of Eleanor Roosevelt reached another turning point.

As usual, she and the children had gone ahead to Campobello for the summer. A few days later Franklin joined them there. Then, with no warning, Franklin fell desperately ill. He could not move his legs. His whole body ached. His fever rose higher and higher. The whole lower part of his body was paralyzed. He could not even sit up.

The Roosevelts' local doctor did not know what was wrong, but a specialist told them the awful truth. Franklin had infantile paralysis—polio—the horrible disease that each year used to cripple thousands of children, and many adults as well. In the summer of 1921, when Franklin became a victim of polio, nobody knew what caused the disease or how to cure it.

For several days it was not certain whether Franklin would live or die. Every breath he took was an agony. And the doctors worried that even if he lived he might never sit up again. In front of Eleanor and the children Franklin never complained. He smiled and even laughed, saying that he would be well in a few days and out on the golf course.

But Eleanor knew that, alone at night, he understood the truth of his situation. One day he had been vigorous and energetic—''the handsome giant,'' as President Wilson had called him, a man whose future seemed so bright. And then, the next day, he was helpless, unable even to move.

Franklin got better. But he never again had

the use of his legs. He had to be lifted and carried from place to place. He had to wear heavy steel braces from his waist to the heels of his shoes.

Still, he refused to think of himself as a cripple. Every day he exercised his chest, neck, arms and shoulders. He became so strong that he easily could hand-wrestle James and the other boys to the ground. He taught himself to crawl on his hands and knees along the floor of his room, so that in case of fire he could escape. Finally, he learned to take a few steps of his own, using crutches.

Franklin's mother saw his illness as a chance to get him under her power again. She hoped that he would give up politics and return to Hyde Park. Once again she talked about his living the life of a country gentleman there, under her personal care.

But he would not even consider it. He would have hated living the life of a sick person, tucked away in the country, inactive, just waiting for death to come.

Eleanor and Louis Howe agreed with him. They helped him stick to his decision, no matter what Mammá said. As Louis insisted, ''By gad, legs or no legs, Franklin will be President.''

Through it all Eleanor managed to stay calm and strong. But sometimes she broke down. Louis once found her slumped in a chair, her head in her hands, totally discouraged. Another time, she was reading aloud to the children and suddenly burst into tears. For a while she couldn't stop crying. So she drenched a towel in cold water and mopped her face with it until she was able to pull herself together again. After that time she almost always was able to control her nerves. She refused ever to cry. But, under such constant self-control, she feared what might happen if that control were to break.

In some ways, Franklin's illness strengthened him. No longer was he just a happy-go-lucky rich man, playing at politics for fun. He became serious. Also, lying flat on his back, he had time to think. He began to consider others who were helpless because of illness, or so poor they had to struggle to stay alive. He started to understand that when people are weak it isn't always their own fault—that sometimes they can't help it. He had more sympathy for people in trouble. And, perhaps for the first time in his life, he could accept different kinds of people, regardless of their looks or their family histories. He was tougher too, with more self-control. Now he could work for many hours without having to stop for play.

Eleanor was stronger, too. At last she had won the struggle with her mother-in-law. Mammá no longer could control Franklin's life, control the children—or Eleanor. Eleanor had stood up to her. And Mammá had backed down. Now, finally, Eleanor was free to live her life as she chose.

Franklin was recovering. But he needed time. Louis Howe told Eleanor that in politics people have short memories; they quickly forget heroes. They might forget about Franklin too. Therefore, said Louis, it was important to keep his name in the public eye. And that meant Eleanor's getting involved in politics herself. According to Louis, it was her duty.

Because of Eleanor's upbringing, the word "duty" meant a great deal to her. She was taught to "do the thing that has to be done, the way it has to be done, when it has to be done." That slogan was drummed into her as a child. After thinking over what Louis had said, she agreed to go ahead. She would go into politics.

Most of Eleanor's work was in New York State, helping to build up the Women's Division of the Democratic State Committee. Her first job was to put out a newspaper, *The Women's Democratic News*. With Louis's help she learned how to prepare a "dummy" of the paper for the printer, how to write headlines, and how to attract advertisers.

Louis arranged for her to make fund-raising speeches all around the state, especially to women's groups. Often she traveled with two women, Nancy Cook and Marion Dickerman, who became her very close friends. Their goal was to set up a Democratic women's club and study group in every county in the state.

Before long Eleanor personally knew more county chairmen and local political leaders than Franklin did. As he grew stronger, she began inviting them to Hyde Park to talk with him.

Besides her work for the Democratic Party, she began to help other groups—the League of Women Voters, the Consumers' League, the Foreign Policy Association and the City Housing Corporation. Once again, she became interested in the problems of working women, especially those served by the Women's Trade Union League (WTUL).

Almost overnight, at the WTUL, Eleanor found herself thrown into contact with a group of remarkable women. Some were immigrants to America, from families with little money. Others, from families like Eleanor's, had given up the idea of living just for their own pleasure. Instead, they were doing exciting work that made a difference in the world.

Social workers Lillian Wald and Mary Simkhovitch, union organizers Rose Schneiderman and Maud Swartz—those women became her friends. They taught her about life in the slums. They once again awakened her hopes that something could be done to make things better.

They—not her wealthy, dull "society" friends—became the center of Eleanor's life. She dropped out of fashionable society. Instead she joined the world of reform—social change.

For hours at a time Eleanor and her reformer friends talked with Franklin. They showed him the need for new laws: laws to get children out of the factories and into schools; to cut down the long hours that women worked; to get fair wages for all workers. They helped to educate him for his future role.

During the years after he was stricken by polio, Eleanor and Franklin spent much of their time at his family estate in Hyde Park, New York.

In other ways too, Eleanor's life began to flower. To speed up her work on the Democratic Party newspaper, she learned typing and shorthand. Next, because Franklin no longer could play with the children as he used to, she decided it was her job. So she learned to swim. She took them camping in Maine and New Hampshire, along with Nancy Cook (who was an excellent camper) and Marion Dickerman. She took them to Europe on a tour. She took them to places in New York, like the museums. And, always, she enjoyed reading aloud to them from books, just as Uncle Theodore had read to her.

In 1926, with Franklin's enthusiastic help—both in money and in architectural planning—Eleanor had a cottage built near the "Big House" at Hyde Park. The cottage, called Val-Kill, was to be a place where Eleanor could relax in privacy with Nancy and Marion, away from the pressures of the world. But it came to take on larger meaning. Both Eleanor and Franklin saw danger in America's becoming a land of city-dwellers. If it were possible, they said, to establish small industries in local areas, then farmers could make part of their living in the countryside. They might not have to leave for the city.

Nancy Cook once had been a woodworking teacher. She suggested that they start a small factory, right in Val-Kill cottage, to make accurate copies of early-American furniture, producing the furniture in the same ways as colonial craftsmen. The three women and Franklin hoped that the project would become a model for rural communities around the country.

In time, Eleanor, Nancy, and Marion became very close. One night Eleanor told them about Franklin's affair with Lucy Mercer and how it had hurt her. Her sharing that secret drew the three women even closer. They became inseparable, missing each other greatly when they were apart. They even had the Val-Kill silverware engraved with the three initials E M N for Eleanor, Marion and Nancy. They did the same for all of their linen (napkins and towels). Val-Kill became, as Franklin smilingly put it, their ''love nest.''

In 1927, again with Franklin's help, Eleanor bought the Todhunter School, a private girls' school in New York City (today known as the Dalton School). Marion became the principal. Eleanor became vice-principal and also taught social studies and literature. Eleanor's model for the school, of course, was Mademoiselle Souvestre's Allenswood. Just as at Allenswood, Eleanor never would let a girl simply parrot the ideas of the textbook. In Eleanor's imagination, she could almost hear Mademoiselle demanding, ''Now that you've repeated what the book says, why not tell us what *you* think?''

She took the Todhunter girls on field trips. They visited police stations, outdoor markets, slums, the courts—anyplace that could show them what life was *really* like outside of their privileged little circle of wealth.

Teaching, Eleanor liked to say, gave her some of the happiest moments in her life. Probably she liked it better than anything else she did.

At Todhunter, the students said a special prayer. It summed up many of the ideas that Eleanor thought were important in life:

> O God, give us clean hands, clean words, clean thoughts. Help us to stand for the hard right against the easy wrong. Save us from habits that harm. Teach us to work as hard and play as fair, in Thy sight alone, as though all the world saw us. Keep us ready to help others and send us chances every day to do a little good and so grow more like Christ. Amen.

By the end of 1927, then, Eleanor had built a whole new life for herself—a life centering on the Todhunter School, Val-Kill, her new friends, and politics.

But in the next year, 1928, all of her freedom, her new independence, would be sorely tested. Once again, she would be called on to behave as the wife of a public official. In November, 1928, Franklin was elected Governor of New York, and the Roosevelts moved to Albany, the state capital.

And an even greater test lay ahead for Eleanor. Just four years later, in 1932, Franklin was elected President of the United States.

7

The Price of Power
(1929–1936)

PROBABLY MOST WOMEN would be pleased to see their husbands elected Governor of New York. But Eleanor had mixed feelings. She was proud that Franklin had won, but unhappy that their friend the former Governor, Al Smith—the first Catholic nominated for the Presidency—had lost his race for President. Most of the other Democrats on the ticket also had lost. More honestly, she thought that now her own active life in politics would end. Once more she would have to play the part of "Franklin Roosevelt's wife." In answer to a reporter's question she snapped peevishly, "No, I am not excited about my husband's election. I don't care. What difference can it make to me?"

She was wrong. Instead of being over, her public life was only beginning.

When Franklin became Governor he often had to visit state institutions—hospitals, parks, prisons, schools. Because of his legs he couldn't get around easily. So he needed Eleanor to be his eyes and ears. At a hospital, for example, she had to inspect the food in the refrigerator, peer behind doors and into closets, see if the beds weren't too crowded together. She talked with the patients—not just the staff—about conditions. Then, remembering every detail, she had to report back to Franklin. He asked hard questions, and at first Eleanor was not a very good reporter. But she learned.

In 1932, when Franklin campaigned for the Presidency, Eleanor made only a few speeches. Still, she did play a part in his victory. She reorganized the Women's Division of the Democratic Party. She also was able to bring together Louis Howe and Jim Farley, the Democratic National Chairman, when they quarreled on how to run the campaign.

The nation that Franklin hoped to lead was in deep trouble. On "Black Thursday," October 24, 1929, prices on the New York Stock Exchange had suddenly tumbled. Thousands of people lost the money they had invested in the stock market. Soon they could not pay their bills or buy new goods. Businesses had to cut down production and lay off workers. Times grew worse and worse. Slowly, the country sank into its deepest depression.

Eleanor herself knew of prosperous families in the suburbs who found themselves reduced to eating stale bread from thrift shops or traveling to parts of town where they were not known to beg for money from house to house. Former executives sold apples on street corners. College professors dug ditches or ran elevators—any jobs they could get. Some people, especially those who never had been poor before, couldn't take the strain, and they committed suicide.

In the winter of 1932–33, as Franklin got ready to take over as President, Eleanor wrote deeply moving accounts of the country's condition. She noted that one of every four Americans was out of work. At mealtimes people stood in long lines in front of soup kitchens for something to eat. Many stuffed newspapers into their jackets and worn-out shoes, trying to keep out the cold. Families who could not pay the rent were turned out of their homes. Often they camped on the edges of our great cities. Sometimes they built makeshift shacks of packing crates, or pounded pieces of old tin into shelters. Eleanor saw their campsites stretching mile after mile along the Hudson River in New York City, right below the elegant apartment houses of Riverside Drive. Their tents dotted the Sheep Meadow in New York's Central Park.

In the countryside, farmers were offered such low prices for their milk that they poured it out on the roads rather than bring it to market. They threw potatoes into the rivers. They let their harvests rot in the fields. And while the harvests rotted, people in the cities sometimes battled each other like dogs for scraps of food left over in restaurant garbage cans.

What Eleanor saw and described was not some poor country in Latin America or Asia or Africa, but the United States—the most prosperous nation in history.

Franklin Roosevelt, sworn in as President in March, 1933, set out to give the people back their confidence. He knew that if the country was to recover, to prosper again, Americans would first have to believe in themselves. When Franklin had been on his back, paralyzed, unable to move, he had known fear, too. He had known terror. But he had overcome it. And so he told the nation on radio, "The only thing we have to fear is fear itself."

Even before Franklin became President, Eleanor was doing what she could to help. She worked at the charity kitchens, ladling out soup. She told her own household staff to have food ready at all times on the stove, and often she sent people to her home for a meal. On the roads, she gave people rides in her car.

Still, Eleanor did not look forward to becoming First Lady and living in the White House. In her mind she pictured herself as "a bird in a gilded cage." She would be admired and protected. She would greet visitors at receptions and preside over official dinners. Yet she would be only a President's wife, with no life of her own. Once she even wrote a letter to Marion Dickerman, telling Marion she couldn't bear the thought of what lay ahead. Nancy Cook saw the letter and showed it to Louis Howe. Louis read it and then ripped it up. He made Nancy swear never to tell Franklin how Eleanor felt. As far as Eleanor knew, Franklin never found out.

Eleanor often enjoyed riding as a morning exercise. On this day, the First Lady rode with the wife of the secretary of state, Mrs. Henry Morgenthau, Jr.

Eleanor understood that feeling sorry for oneself helps nothing. She decided that, as much as possible, she would live in Washington as "just plain Eleanor Roosevelt," not as First Lady. But she would also be useful to Franklin.

She would go out into the country and listen to what people were saying. Then she would report back to Franklin. He would know what actually was going on, not just what his advisers wanted him to know. By then, she was an experienced observer. Franklin trusted her judgment, and he listened to her.

Meanwhile, Eleanor had made a new friend, an Associated Press reporter named Lorena Hickok. "Hick," as people called her, seemed to understand Eleanor better than anyone else. And Eleanor could trust her. She could tell Lorena her innermost thoughts. Lorena gave her a sapphire ring which she looked at often, and when she did she would think of Lorena. When they were together they read poetry aloud to each other. When they were apart Eleanor missed her and would even kiss her picture.

Hick knew that Eleanor still suffered a deep hurt from Franklin's romance with Lucy Mercer. She knew, too, that although Eleanor could no longer love Franklin as before, she was deeply loyal to him. He depended on her. And Eleanor wanted to help him in his work, to be his partner. Hick helped Eleanor to realize that now in helping Franklin she also had a chance to help the country.

The first things Eleanor did were right inside the White House. It was to be "home" for the Roosevelt family, and, without taking away from its dignity, she wanted it to be a warm, friendly, informal place. Some of the Roosevelt children were grown and independent. But John and Franklin, Jr., often were home, and always there were many active grandchildren, bursting with energy, as one might expect of Roosevelt children. For the first time since Uncle Ted and his family occupied the White House one could hear the laughter of young children at play. On the third floor Eleanor had nursery rooms put in, and on the south lawn a sandbox and a jungle gym for climbing. She even had an old-fashioned swing put up on one of the trees.

Always there was much to do. In Eleanor's first year in the White House she received more than 300,000 pieces of mail. She answered thousands of the letters herself. Visitors to the White House also took time. Once she shook the hands of 3,100 members of the Daughters of the American Revolution in just an hour and a half. During the year 1939 alone, 4,729 people came for meals and 9,211 came for tea.

Over the years Eleanor grew to understand that people expected to meet her. They wanted to see the President's wife, and doing so helped tie them closer to their government. The White House, after all, is the "people's house." But being a hostess was part of the job of First Lady that Eleanor did not really enjoy.

One crowded day followed another. And Eleanor tried to face each day with calmness and serenity. She tried to accept life, and to take things as they came along.

The Depression, it seemed to her, was, of course, a horror, but one that could be turned to good advantage. She thought that people would now have to learn to cooperate. They would have to learn to want less for themselves and more for their fellow humans. They would have to learn to share, to be less selfish, to work together in a common cause. The result could well be a new kind of civilization—one built on cooperation instead of competition and struggle.

In that new world, everyone would have enough food, enough clothing, good shelter. No man would have to steal a loaf of bread to stay alive and to feed his children as so often happened in the Depression. But first, each person would have to stop thinking so much about what he could get for himself and start thinking about others.

Eleanor had immensely enjoyed teaching at the Todhunter School. Now, as First Lady, the entire nation could be her classroom. She could speak out on her own. She could try to help people face their problems. But that depended on putting her ideas simply. She had to give concrete examples from daily life that men and women in trouble could understand and actually use. And she had to do it without preaching—because people get tired of being preached to. Her teaching would have to be by the example of her life and the way she lived it.

At Lorena Hickok's suggestion, Eleanor held weekly press conferences to answer the questions of women reporters. She began to write a newspaper column, called "My Day." She had her own radio program. She traveled around the country, lecturing to large audiences, often on topics that interested women—child care, life in the White House, the work of women in politics.

It was satisfying for Eleanor to be so busy to

have her mind filled with new plans, new activities. She discovered that by being interested in other people she could find greater happiness for herself. She was, moreover, being recognized, becoming known for things that she herself was doing, not just for being Franklin's wife.

People sometimes liked to joke about her traveling so much. They laughed about a woman—and especially a First Lady—showing up in such unlikely places. Once she went high in the air in the cabin of one of the enormous cranes being used to build a dam in the Tennessee River Valley. She put on overalls and went underground into the coal mines to talk to miners in Pennsylvania, West Virginia and Ohio. Admiral Byrd, who explored Antarctica, teased that in his hut near the South Pole he set an extra place at supper, just in case she decided to drop in.

Eleanor didn't mind the teasing. The only way she could know what people were feeling was to visit them. That meant being with automotive assembly-line workers in Detroit, or the wives and children of migrant farm workers in California, or unemployed young

As the Depression worsened, Eleanor began traveling extensively to be with the poor and unemployed. In 1936 she visited coal-mining communities in Ohio, Pennsylvania, and West Virginia.

people in Manhattan, or housewives in Midwestern suburbs. She had to go to them. It was her responsibility, and also it was what she really wanted to do.

Once Eleanor visited a coal-mining community in West Virginia. In one cabin a family of six had only scraps to eat, the kind of leftovers one might give to a dog. As she was about to leave, two of the children, a boy and a girl, waited for her by the door. The little boy held a pet rabbit in his arms. His sister, thin and scrawny, looked up at Eleanor and said, "He thinks we're not going to eat it, but we are." At that, the little boy fled down the road, holding the rabbit closer than ever. That incident, Eleanor remarked, illustrated what poverty is all about.[*]

Franklin had a name for his plan to help America conquer the Depression. He called it the New Deal. He said that Americans who were without jobs, without hope for the future, deserved a fresh start, a new shuffling of the deck—a "new deal." While he tried to get Congress to pass laws that would help people, Eleanor had an assignment, too. She tried to show, by visiting those who were suffering most, that someone very close to the President knew about their problems—and cared.

The American people must have believed that Franklin was trying, and succeeding. In the election of 1936 he won a landslide victory, carrying all but two states.

Still, the Depression was far from over. And, overseas, the leaders of Germany, Italy and Japan were beginning to bully and threaten the countries around them. Those

[*]Adapted from Eleanor Roosevelt, *This I Remember* (New York: Harper and Brothers, 1949).

men—who hoped to conquer the world—came to be an even greater danger to America's survival than the Depression.

What they did would have an enormous impact, too, on the life of Eleanor Roosevelt.

8

First Lady in Peace and War (1937–1945)

IN HER YOUTH, and even as an adult, Eleanor Roosevelt had prejudices. When she was unsure of herself, shy, she felt safer with people who were like her—people of the same race, the same religion, the same social class.

As she grew older, she learned that people are both good and bad. They are intelligent or unintelligent. They are kind or they are cruel. But it is not because they are blacks or Jews or Italians or English. Eleanor learned to see each person as a person, not as a member of some group.

In greeting or saying goodbye to people, she liked to kiss them. There was a time, however, when it was painful for her to do that with blacks, even her good friend Mary Mc-Leod Bethune, one of America's outstanding black leaders. When the time came that Eleanor could kiss Mary without any special thought, she knew that she had overcome her prejudice.

Once, in 1939, Eleanor went to a meeting with Mary in Birmingham, Alabama. In much of the South in those days blacks were kept separate from whites. When the police told her that she had to sit on the "whites only" side of the auditorium it made her very angry. She thought that it was absurd to sort out people by their skin color. So she picked up her chair and put it down right in the middle of the aisle separating blacks and whites.

That pleased many of her black friends. But it angered many whites, and some of them wrote to Franklin to complain about her. Franklin always liked to say, "I may be President of the United States, but I can't tell Eleanor what to do or what to think."

A few weeks later the D.A.R. (Daughters of the American Revolution) would not let the great black singer Marian Anderson perform in their large auditorium in Washington, D.C., Constitution Hall. They said that they did not allow blacks there. The D.A.R. is a patriotic organization whose members all must prove that their ancestors played a part in the American Revolution. For many years Eleanor had been a member of the D.A.R., but when she heard what they had done to Marian Anderson she resigned. Then she arranged to have Miss Anderson sing in front of the Lincoln Memorial. It was a huge outdoor concert, with more than 75,000 people lining the Mall from the Lincoln Memorial to the Washington Monument. Marian Anderson began by singing "America," but she ended with a song whose words many blacks in our country have understood by experience—"Nobody Knows the Trouble I've Seen."

Sometimes Eleanor became impatient with Franklin for moving so slowly to make things better for the underdogs in American life—those who always seem to be used by the rich and privileged. Blacks in particular were suffering. They were separated from whites in the armed forces, where there were very few black officers. Blacks did not have equal opportunities for jobs. What jobs they could get usually paid low wages and gave little chance for advancement—such as being porters on railroad trains or bellhops in hotels.

President Roosevelt knew how Eleanor felt

about these injustices, but he reminded her that, as President, he had to please many people, including many in the South, where some of the worst acts of prejudice were taking place. He needed the votes of Southern congressmen, he pointed out to Eleanor, to get laws passed that the entire nation needed.

Eleanor, however, spoke only for herself—not, as Franklin did, for the whole Democratic Party or for the whole nation. So she was free to take stronger stands. She could even say things that many Americans at that time did not like to hear. For example, she said that laws were wrong that kept blacks and whites separate in schools, theaters, restaurants, and other public places. She could write that blacks deserved better opportunities for good jobs and good housing. As she had done in Marian Anderson's conflict with the D.A.R., Eleanor could speak out firmly against prejudice and snobbery.

In some people's eyes that made Eleanor look firm and forceful; it made Franklin look weak and wishy-washy. The story is told that Eleanor's cousin Alice Roosevelt Longworth once said that Franklin was "one part mush and three parts Eleanor." Just as when Alice and Eleanor were children, Alice kept on saying cruel things. She liked to do an act in which she would make fun of the way Eleanor walked and talked. Then, one evening after dinner at the White House, Eleanor asked her to do the act in front of everyone. After that, she stopped doing it.

Princess Alice was only one member of the Roosevelt family. Eleanor thought about, and worried about, the others too. By the middle of the 1930s her younger brother, Hall, had begun drinking heavily. He and his wife divorced. Then one of his sons committed suicide. Another son was killed in a plane crash. Eleanor tried to protect Hall—save him from himself. But despite great charm and intelligence, he had little self-control and went deeper and deeper into drink.

Eleanor's own children turned to her in times of trouble. James, Elliott and Anna all married young, only to have their marriages end in divorce. Eleanor wanted them to know that, whatever happened, they always would be welcomed at home. She accepted them, Franklin, Jr., for example, often was stopped by the police for speeding, and Eleanor once insisted that Franklin, Sr., take away his driver's license. But when he was taken to the hospital after an accident Eleanor rushed to his side. In 1938, when James nearly died in an operation on his stomach, both the President and Mrs. Roosevelt flew to the Mayo Clinic in Rochester, Minnesota, to be with him.

Eleanor believed that children should be allowed their own opinions. As a result, the Roosevelt dinner table usually was the scene of lively debates. Even after the children left home, the discussions continued. As a radio commentator in Texas, Elliott often criticized his father's policies. In 1937 Franklin, Jr., married Ethel du Pont, a daughter of a family that had supplied vast amounts of money for attacks on President Roosevelt's New Deal.

Franklin, as President of the United States, could not always leave the White House when the children were in trouble. So the burden fell on Eleanor. She tried to help. But, remembering the lesson of Sara Roosevelt's interference in her personal life, Eleanor stayed out of her children's affairs as much as possible. At the same time, she let them know that she loved them and cared about what was happening to them.

During the Roosevelt's second four years in the White House the Depression hung on. People still were without jobs. In spite of ev-

Eleanor Roosevelt was an admired and influential supporter of humanitarian causes. Here, in Washington, DC, she passed out Christmas gifts to needy children.

erything Franklin had done, he had to admit that one third of the nation was still "ill-housed, ill-clothed, and ill-fed."

With the problem of poverty still unsolved, yet another great menace arose—the danger of war.

All through the 1930s the United States, Great Britain and the other democracies thought of little else but fighting the Depression. Meanwhile, the Japanese invaded Manchuria and China. Benito Mussolini sent his Italian soldiers into the helpless African nation of Ethiopia. Adolf Hitler's brutal German forces marched into the Rhineland, then Austria, then Czechoslovakia.

Early in life Eleanor had been a pacifist. She was against war altogether. War, it seemed to her, was completely wasteful, senseless. It never settled anything properly, and usually a nation was worse off going to war than not. But as Eleanor looked around the world in the 1930s she saw that peace-loving nations, like China during that period, simply could not protect themselves. They were morally right, but too weak. And in the end they were conquered, their people enslaved.

Eleanor began to see that if we, the free people of the world, were to survive we would have to pull together. To Eleanor and Franklin, England looked like America's strongest friend in the defense of freedom. To help strengthen ties with that country, the Roosevelts invited King George VI and Queen Elizabeth of England to America for a visit. During their stay in June, 1939, Eleanor and Franklin entertained them at their home, Hyde Park. Some

In June 1939, the Roosevelts invited Britain's King George VI (second from left) and Queen Elizabeth (second from right) to Hyde Park.

newspapers were angry that, on being introduced to the Queen, Eleanor did not kneel. Others criticized her because, for a picnic at Hyde Park, she served simple things like hot dogs, potato salad and ice cream to the royal guests. But the King and Queen felt very much at home with the Roosevelts. It was a good visit.

Young people, Eleanor thought, had a special part to play in keeping America strong and alert. She particularly liked the young people in the American Youth Congress—teenagers and college students who frequently raised their voices against Hitler. She helped them in every way she could, speaking at their meetings, letting them list her name on their stationery as a sponsor, writing for their newspaper. But when Soviet troops invaded tiny, defenseless Finland, the leaders of the Youth Congress made excuses for the Russians. They did not seem to understand, she said, that evil is evil, whether it is done in the name of German Nazism or Russian Communism.

Eleanor told the Youth Congress they no longer could expect her help. She never again let them use her name. Still, many of them remained her friends. She liked them as people and enjoyed their company. And she was pleased to see that some of them later realized how the Russians had used them as tools.

In September, 1939, Hitler invaded Poland. Then he conquered Denmark, Norway, the Netherlands and Belgium. France fell. Only Great Britain remained free.

One of Eleanor's classmates at Allenswood, Carola, now Mrs. Carola von Schaeffer-Bernstein, had returned to her German homeland after living in England. She wrote to Eleanor with pride about the sense of purpose that

Hilter and the other new leaders had given to German life. To Carola, it was a matter of joy that her son would serve in the German Army. Through politeness for a friend Eleanor did not remind her of what Mademoiselle Souvestre certainly would have thought of the ruthless, cruel and cowardly things Adolf Hitler was doing.

What would be America's response to Hitler? President Roosevelt saw the danger and wanted the country to get ready for war, before it was too late—as it had been for the countries of Europe. But many Americans, as Eleanor observed, thought that getting ready was a mistake, as if doing nothing—putting our heads in the sand like ostriches—would make the danger go away.

Eleanor saw in this crisis, as she had in the Depression, a chance for improvement. She hoped that the whole nation would join together in a tremendous effort. Every American, she thought, should do something— young and old, men and women, black and white. We should have a body-building program for everyone. There should be training for all in first aid, nutrition, health habits. Every person should be asked to share the burden and make sacrifices. And the more that was asked of them, it seemed to Eleanor, the prouder they would be of their country. As she had learned in her own life, people like to feel needed. They like to be part of some enterprise larger than themselves.

As the election of 1940 came closer, the world situation grew more desperate. To many people, Germany, Italy and Japan looked invincible—unbeatable. Nothing could stop them from conquering the world. Franklin believed that in such troubled times the country needed his qualities of leadership. He decided to run for a third term as President, something that no President ever had done before.

The Democratic Party chose him as its candidate. But at the party convention many Democrats disapproved of Franklin's choice for Vice-President, Henry A. Wallace, considering him too liberal. The party leaders asked Eleanor to speak to the convention and do what she could to help Wallace.

As she rose to speak the delegates were in wild disorder. Eleanor approached the rostrum slowly, walking as straight and tall as she could. She had no notes but had carefully thought out what she would say.

For a few seconds she waited for silence, and, as if by magic, a hush came over the auditorium. Then she spoke, talking about responsibility—the tremendous responsibility of each person in such dangerous times to do what had to be done. Eleanor talked about Franklin's great burden—his responsibility as President and how he needed everyone's help and support.

When she finished, the organist began softly playing "God Bless America." Then the cheering started. Perhaps Eleanor's speech helped, because, before long, the convention overwhelmingly nominated Mr. Wallace.

Franklin won the election of 1940. Yet for many months afterward the debate about the war continued to rage. Should the United States stay neutral—on the sidelines? Should America help Great Britain with arms and ammunition? The argument was ripping the nation apart.

Then, suddenly, the discussion stopped. On Sunday, December 7, 1941, the Japanese attacked America's naval base at Pearl Harbor, Hawaii. The next day, Franklin asked Congress for a declaration of war.

Overnight, a badly divided country united behind Franklin Roosevelt. Even some of those who had opposed him every step of the way on the road to preparedness cheered him wildly. In that moment, Americans were angry and afraid. And he was their leader.

For Eleanor, the years that followed were bitter. All four of her sons were in the armed forces: Elliott in the Air Force, James in the Marines, and Franklin, Jr., and John in the Navy. Meanwhile, Franklin's mother had died, just before Pearl Harbor. Perhaps, mused Eleanor, it was well that she didn't live to see her world—with its old values—swept away by change.

Eleanor's younger brother, Hall, also died. As with his father, it was alcohol that killed him. At the time of Hall's death Eleanor expressed a wish that all youngsters who drank and abused their health could see what happened to him, a boy of great promise whose life had been largely wasted. In Eleanor's memory, Hall, from childhood, had put off unpleasant things, taken the easy way out. He had been without self-discipline, self-control. Those were qualities that had made Eleanor a woman of enormous strength.

But in those days there was little time to grieve for the dead. Eleanor had a job to do for the living. She sold war bonds, gave blood, helped the Red Cross raise money, knitted sweaters and socks for servicemen. Early in the war she visited American soldiers at their camps in England. She toured the hospitals, spoke to British women, and met with the British Prime Minister Winston Churchill. She also saw firsthand how modern warfare could turn whole parts of a great city like London into rubble.

In 1943 she crossed the Pacific, a trip of 25,000 miles. Americans were fighting on dozens of jungle islands, meeting fierce Japanese resistance. Whenever possible Eleanor ate with the enlisted men, not just the officers. That was how she could tell Franklin what was needed: better food, the right kinds of clothing and, most important of all, faster mail service.

When Eleanor visited a hospital she stopped at every bed. To each soldier she said something special, usually something that a mother might say. Often, after she left, even battle-hardened men had tears in their eyes. At first, Admiral Halsey had considered her visit a nui-

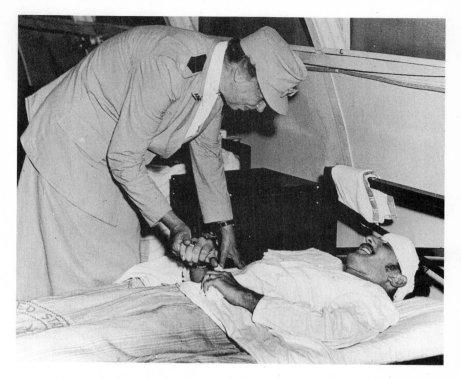

In 1943, Eleanor traveled 25,000 miles through 17 Pacific islands, visiting with enlisted men in hospitals and military bases.

sance. But by the time she was ready to leave for the United States he had become one of her strongest admirers. Nobody else, he said, had done so much to help raise the spirits of the men.

At night after an entire day of visiting hospitals, recovery centers, and barracks, she sat down at her typewriter and prepared her newspaper column. She had agreed to continue writing, especially during her travels, as a way of linking women at home to their loved ones overseas. In all the years that Eleanor wrote her column, "My Day," she never once missed a deadline.

As the election of 1944 approached, Franklin voiced a wish that he would not have to run again. He knew that the strain of being President was shortening his life. And now he was noticeably tired, worn thin. But even more than in 1940—when he had decided to try for a third term—he felt it was his duty to go on.

He won the election. But as the days passed Eleanor could almost see him grow more weary. Working hard herself, she could not bring him the lightness and gaiety he needed, the relief from his burdens. She was too serious about her own activities for that, too absorbed in getting things done.

Once, while she was away traveling, Lucy Mercer Rutherfurd came to the White House for dinner. Anna, Eleanor's daughter, was there. Anna knew how much Franklin's old romance with Lucy had hurt her mother. She also knew how hard Eleanor had worked to patch the marriage together. Franklin knew, too. They did not tell Eleanor about Mrs.

Rutherfurd's visit. They brought her to the White House behind Eleanor's back.

By spring, 1945, the end of the war in Europe seemed near. The Germans clearly could not hold out much longer. Franklin had gone to Warm Springs, Georgia, for a rest. Then, on the afternoon of April 12, a phone call brought the news.

Franklin was dead. Eleanor later learned that Lucy Mercer Rutherfurd had been with him at the end.

Somehow, the death of Franklin—a strong leader, a world hero—seemed a greater loss to the nation than to Eleanor personally. After all, as she explained, she could go on. She was strong. She could adjust to life as she always had. But the problems facing the country were enormous.

Eleanor later said that Franklin might have been happier with a different wife—a wife who did not argue with him so much, one who would praise him, as his mother had done, please him, say ''yes'' to all of his ideas. That Eleanor was never able to do, and he had to find it in other people. Still, declared Eleanor, ''I think that sometimes I acted as his conscience. I urged him to take the harder path when he would have preferred the easier way. In that sense, I acted on occasion as a spur, even though the spurring was not always wanted or welcome.''

''In living his life,'' said Eleanor, ''Franklin had a pattern in mind, a plan. No one person could have done everything for him. Like his mother, and Louis Howe, and Lucy Mercer Rutherfurd, I happened to be one of those who served his purposes.''

''Of course,'' she said, ''I loved him, and I miss him.''

After Franklin's funeral, every day that Eleanor was home at Hyde Park, without fail, she placed flowers on his grave. Then she would stand very still beside him there.

9

On Her Own (after 1945)

WHEN FRANKLIN DIED, Eleanor was sixty-one years old. True, she had a clear mind, great energy, and friends she had come to know and love. Nevertheless, she thought that her public life was over. Still unsure of herself, she believed that after Franklin's death she would no longer be news. People would lose interest in her. Probably she would drop out of the public eye and be remembered in the history books only as a footnote to the New Deal era.

But that didn't happen. She discovered that there still was much work that she could do, there were many people she could help. She found new sources of strength within herself and new ways to live a useful, interesting life—a life of fulfillment. Now, moreover, she was able to be herself. Her successes were her own, not those of ''the President's wife.''

Just as Franklin wished, soon after his death Eleanor turned the ''Big House'' at Hyde Park over to the government. It became a museum and library where people could come to learn about his life. They could see the house exactly as it was when he and Eleanor had lived there.

By 1945, Eleanor's friends Nancy Cook and Marion Dickerman had moved out of the cottage at Val-Kill, and she took that for herself. She entertained visitors there: Chiang Kai-shek of China, Princess Juliana of the Netherlands, Ambassador Gromyko of the Soviet Union and others. But most of the time she lived in an apartment on Washington Square in Manhattan's Greenwich Village. Lorena Hickok, her reporter friend, helped her get the apartment ready and sometimes stayed there with her.

Everywhere Eleanor went people recognized her. But that was easy to understand. She had been First Lady for more than twelve years, through the crisis of depression and then of war. Unlike other wives of Presidents, she hadn't stayed home in the White House.

She had traveled. She had been photographed for newspapers and appeared in movie newsreels. Besides, her looks made her easy to recognize. As a result, it was hard for her to live a private life. Outside her apartment in New York she couldn't go for a loaf of bread or down to the subway without being stopped by somebody.

But she remembered that if being well known had its price, it also had its rewards. Being Eleanor Roosevelt made it possible for her to get many things done in the world that she saw needed to be done.

About eight months after Franklin died President Harry S. Truman invited Eleanor to be one of the American delegates going to London to begin the work of the United Nations.

"Why me?" she asked him. Surely there were many people who knew more about law and politics and world affairs. But the President insisted, and Eleanor agreed.

When it was announced that she was to be a delegate, John Foster Dulles (later an American Secretary of State) called the choice "terrible." But soon, after watching her at work, he admitted he had been wrong. She proved her-

After Franklin's death, Eleanor continued in public life. She served (1945-52 and 1961-62) as a U.S. delegate to the United Nations and helped draft the U.N. Declaration of Human Rights.

self to be a hard bargainer, a strong speaker for America's ideas, and a person who always was prepared—she "did her homework."

Mrs. Roosevelt's first assignment was with the United Nations committee on social, cultural and humanitarian affairs. Those were the kinds of supposedly unimportant things, men thought, that would interest a woman— and where she could do the least harm.

To everyone's surprise a hot fight developed in the committee. Since the beginning of World War II the Soviet Union had sent its armies into neighboring countries, eventually overrunning much of Eastern Europe. By 1945 the countries under direct or indirect control of the Soviets included Latvia, Estonia, Lithuania, Hungary, Czechoslovakia, Poland, Rumania, Bulgaria and East Germany. The Soviet Union demanded that people who had left their home countries during the war be returned. But, as Eleanor learned, many of those people did not want to return to Russia, or to nations that the Soviet Union ruled. They wanted to be free to make their own choices.

Andrei Vishinsky spoke for the Soviets. He made a long summary speech, so that it was nearly 3 A.M. when Eleanor's time came. In just a few words she said that people should have the right to choose for themselves; nobody should be forced to return to his homeland against his will. The vote was taken, and Eleanor's position won.

Still, she made certain not to "rub in" the defeat. Individuals, like nations, Eleanor believed, should be able to disagree, to differ, without turning to violence. At a party celebrating her seventieth birthday Eleanor was pleased to welcome Andrei Vishinsky as an honored personal guest.

Mrs. Roosevelt later served as chairperson of the United Nations Commission for Human Rights. The commission's task was to write a Declaration of Human Rights—something like America's Declaration of Independence and Bill of Rights, but for all the people of the world. The Soviets wanted the Declaration to tell what duties people owed to their countries in return for education, health care and jobs. But Eleanor, like most Americans, wanted the Declaration to talk about the individual's rights and freedoms, such as freedom of speech and freedom of religion. The needs of people, she said, came before the needs of governments.

For many months the commission members argued. At last, they compromised. Everyone gave in a little. And the General Assembly of the United Nations accepted their Declaration of Human Rights almost exactly as they had written it. Without Eleanor's hard work and patience almost certainly there would have been no Declaration of Human Rights. She was, to some U.N. delegates, the Declaration's "mother."

In 1953, when Dwight D. Eisenhower, a Republican, became President, Eleanor resigned her position at the United Nations so that Eisenhower could choose his own representative. As the election of 1960 approached she came to know John F. Kennedy, the Democratic Party's candidate for the Presidency. She considered him brilliant, a young man who could inspire, who could show the world what America stands for not particular economic system or miracle of production, but a basis belief in the dignity of mankind and the worth of the individual.

Kennedy, she said, was strong enough to admit that America still had serious problems—and to care that around the globe too many people's lives were twisted, warped, by poverty. The values of Western civilization, said Eleanor, needed to be stated in ringing tones. It was those beliefs that made us different from the Communists, as, before, they had made us different from the Nazis. And it was those same values, if we could hold to them, that would overcome the Soviet threat.

Still, she said, it was important to keep talking to one's opponents and to learn to understand them. Not to do those things, said Mrs. Roosevelt, was sheer madness. Despite public criticism, she visited Soviet Premier Nikita Khrushchev overseas, and when he came to the United States she had him to tea at Hyde Park as her guest.

In 1961 President Kennedy appointed Eleanor once again as a delegate to the United Nations. As she arrived to take her seat the delegates from the other nations gave her a standing ovation. It was something that never before had happened at the U.N. and was one of the proudest moments of her life.

Eleanor Roosevelt, said one delegate, is "a tall pillar of a quality no one else in our time has produced."

All along, Eleanor's doctor had been telling her to slow down. But that was hard for her. She was a person who liked to say "Yes" to life. She thought that life was meant to be lived, and that one should never, for whatever reason, turn his back on it.

Even in old age Eleanor still wrote books and articles. She lectured all across the country. She even did a regular television program. Every summer she gave a picnic at Hyde Park for the boys of the Wiltwyck School, who are emotionally disturbed. She would let them swim in the pool and then would fill them full of hot dogs, potato salad, popcorn and ice cream. After that, she would read aloud to them from Rudyard Kipling's *Just So Stories*, just as she always had to her own children. And they listened.

After Franklin's death, Eleanor's travels took her around the world—to Syria, Lebanon, Jordan, Israel, Morocco, India, Pakistan, Thailand, Japan, Greece, Turkey, Yugoslavia, the Soviet Union. Everywhere, she met people who were as eager to greet her as she was to see them. Although, as a girl, she was brought up to be formal, distant, she felt at ease with those people. They wanted to touch her, to hug her, to kiss her. And she did not mind. They reached out to her, and she returned their love.

Always, too, there was home—the cottage at Val-Kill. She loved to be there to see the winter snows and to see the dogwood trees

Even in old age, Eleanor still wrote books, lectured, and traveled around the world as a tireless worker for social causes.

bloom in the spring. She swam in the same pool where Franklin used to swim.

Her children, of course, were very dear to her. Through the years their lives were not always happy, and she sorrowed for them. But she tried not to interfere. It never seemed right to her that a parent should give advice; each person must live his own life. Still, it was hard for her to resist being a mother. One night she sat beside her son James on a speaker's platform during dinner. He was over fifty years old at the time, but that didn't stop her from leaning over to him and whispering that he should eat his peas.

In time, she no longer was able to ride her horse, Dot, along the trails near Val-Kill, and long ago she had stopped playing tennis. But she adored having her grandchildren gathered around her. Sometimes friends from the New Deal days would come to call. And even a few old friends from her girlhood still survived. They called her "Totty," remembering the days of their youth.

President Truman once referred to her as the "First Lady of the World." She liked that. But in the time that was left to her she claimed to prefer something a little less grand. "I'm still a tough old bird," as she put it, "and I'm prepared to face whatever comes along. That is because, with age, I have learned to accept myself, to be at peace with myself. Now, all I hope for is that I can meet the future with courage and with the best that I have to give.''

On November 7, 1962, Eleanor Roosevelt died in her sleep. She was buried in the rose garden at Hyde Park, alongside her husband, Franklin.

Chronology

1884   Anna Eleanor Roosevelt is born.

1890   Mother dies. Theodore Roosevelt appointed guardian. Father dies.

1894   Eleanor goes to England to attend Allenswood School.

1902   Eleanor makes her debut; joins the Junior League and works at Rivington Street Settlement House.

1903   Eleanor marries Franklin D. Roosevelt.

1906   Children, Anna Eleanor, James, Franklin Jr.,
-1916   Elliot, another Franklin Jr., and John are born.

1910   FDR elected to New York State Senate.

1913   FDR appointed Assistant Secretary of the Navy.

1918   Eleanor discovers FDR's affair with Lucy Mercer.

1920   FDR nominated for Vice President. Eleanor makes friends with Louis Howe.

1921   FDR contracts polio. Eleanor becomes active in New York State Democratic politics; meets Nancy Cook and Marion Dickerman.

1926   Eleanor plans and builds Val-Kill.

1927   Eleanor buys Todhunter School in New York City.

1928   Eleanor is "eyes and ears" for FDR campaign for Governor.

1932   Eleanor works in FDR's campaign; acts as peacemaker.

1933   FDR inaugurated. Eleanor meets Lorena Hickok; begins writing "My Day."

1939   Eleanor helps to arrange Marian Anderson concert at Lincoln Memorial.

1941   Japanese attack Pearl Harbor.

1943   Eleanor makes 25,000 mile tour of Pacific battle fields.

1945   FDR dies. Eleanor moves to Val-Kill; attends London conference on the United Nations; works of the Declaration of Human Rights.

1953   Eleanor resigns from the United Nations.

1961   President John Kennedy appoints Eleanor to the United Nations.

1962   Eleanor dies and is buried at Hyde Park.

For Further Reading

The most useful way to learn about Eleanor Roosevelt is to read her own words. She wrote several books, including *This Is My Story* (1937), *This I Remember* (1949), and *On My Own* (1958). In those books, as well as in her one-volume *Autobiography of Eleanor Roosevelt* (1960), Mrs. Roosevelt speaks of her life and her ideas, often with great frankness.

The Roosevelt children have written about their parents in intimate detail. See, for example, Elliott Roosevelt's *Mother R: Eleanor Roosevelt's Untold Story* (1977) and James Roosevelt's *My Parents: A Differing View* (1976).

The story of Eleanor's close friendship with Marion Dickerman and Nancy Cook is told in Kenneth Davis's *Invincible Summer: An Intimate*

Portrait of the Roosevelts (1974). For her special relationship with Lorena Hickok see Miss Hickok's *Reluctant First Lady* (1962), Doris Faber's biography, *The Life of Lorena Hickok, E.R.'s Friend* (1980), and Joseph P. Lash's definitive study, *Love, Eleanor* (1982).

Many biographies of Eleanor Roosevelt appeared shortly after her death and are essentially tributes in her memory. The best of these are actress/politician Helen Gahagan Douglas's *The Eleanor Roosevelt We Remember* (1963) and the moving sketch by poet Archibald MacLeish, *The Eleanor Roosevelt Story* (1965).

Clearly, however, the outstanding biographies of Mrs. Roosevelt are two sensitive, thoroughly researched works by Joseph P. Lash, *Eleanor and Franklin* (1971) and *Eleanor: The Years Alone* (1972). They are based on the careful examination of thousands of boxes of Eleanor's papers and many interviews with people who knew her, as did Lash himself. The present writer is particularly indebted to the information and insights contained in Lash's extraordinary studies.

Index